TO:

FROM:

Copyright © 2009 Hallmark Licensing, Inc.

Published by Hallmark Books,
a division of Hallmark Cards, Inc.,
Kansas City, MO 64141
Visit us on the Web at www.Hallmark.com.

Editorial Director: Todd Hafer
Writer: Kevin Dilmore
Editor: Theresa Trinder
Art Director: Kevin Swanson
Illustrator: Tom Patrick
Designer: Mark Voss
Production Artist: Dan Horton

ISBN: 978-1-59530-202-1

BOK4349

Printed and bound in the United States of America

SUPERDAD

AND HIS
DARING DADVENTURES

CREATED BY KEVIN DILMORE & TOM PATRICK

GIFT BOOKS
from Hallmark

CAPED WONDER STUNS NEIGHBORHOOD

In a surprise show of super heroics, a man known only as Superdad made his public debut in a residential neighborhood yesterday, rescuing several people from injury— or worse.

The caped mystery man, wearing a colorful costume complete with hood and goggles to protect his identity, arrived in the nick of time to assist people caught in yesterday's severe weather.

A surprise thunderstorm with winds reaching 50 mph swept through a southside neighborhood, threatening a man repairing his roof and a group of children building a treehouse.

"He was amazing. I've never seen anyone like Superdad," said one neighbor.

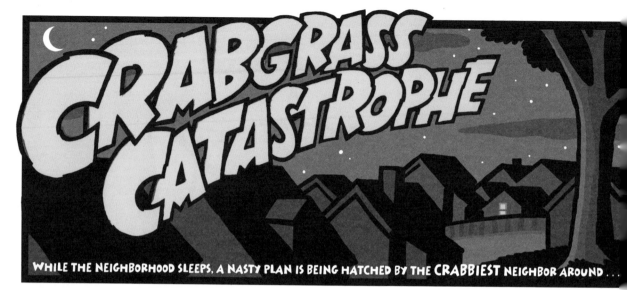

THE TECHNO GOGGLES

I'm not sleeping. I'm resting my eyes!

NIGHT VISION

TELESCOPIC VISION

X-RAY VISION

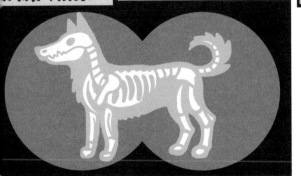

DADA-LINK TO DADA-COMPUTER

MARTIN, AGE 9

ALIASES:
MARTY,
SON

LIKES:
THROWING STUFF,
VIDEO GAMES,
DOGS,
HOT DOGS

WHIZZER, AGE 14
(DOG YEARS)

ALIASES:
GOOD BOY,
BAD DOG

LIKES:
CATCHING STUFF,
SLEEPING,
PEOPLE,
PEOPLE FOOD

THE TURBO TOOL
SUPER SCREWDRIVER (PHILLIPS, FLATHEAD, AND HEX SOCKET!)
Big job or small, it's one tool for all!
THUNDER HAMMER (WATCH YOUR THUMBS!)
ROBO WRENCH (HECK YEAH, IT'S A RATCHET!)
BALLISTIC BOTTLE OPENER (BECAUSE YOU NEVER KNOW!)

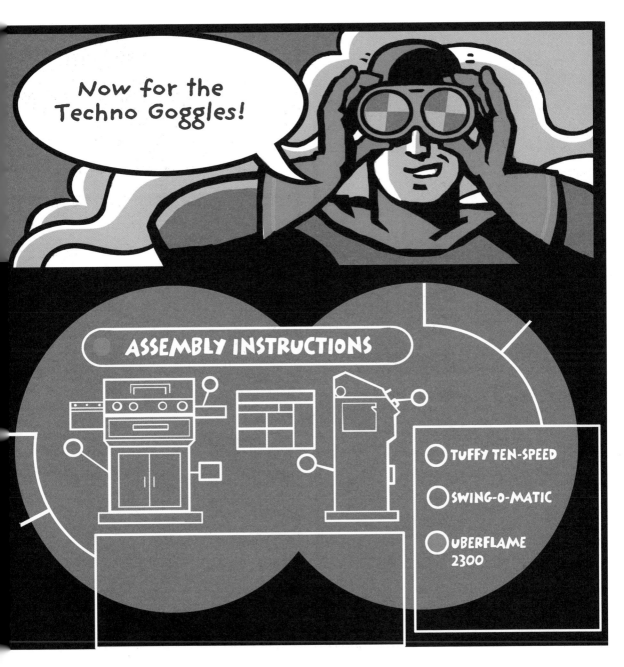

Follow the instructions, kids, and you won't get burned!
SD
THE END
OR IS IT?
BZZZT

WHO IS SUPERDAD?

Hey, where did Superdad come from?

Yeah, what's his story?

Well, kids...

"SOME SAY HE WAS BORN TO GREATNESS."

He'll make a SUPER dad someday!

"OTHERS SAY HE LEARNED EARLY."

I'm doing it by myself!

"AND THEN ONE DAY, HE ANSWERED THE CALL TO PROTECT AND SERVE THE NEIGHBORHOOD."

But what about his powers?

And all his cool stuff?

"SOME THINK ALIEN TECHNOLOGY IS INVOLVED..."

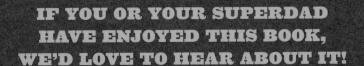

**IF YOU OR YOUR SUPERDAD
HAVE ENJOYED THIS BOOK,
WE'D LOVE TO HEAR ABOUT IT!**

Please send your comments to:
Hallmark Book Feedback
P.O. Box 419034
Mail Drop 215
Kansas City, MO 64141

Or e-mail us at:
booknotes@hallmark.com